Love . . .
from the Animals

Karen Bentley DVM, RHom

BALBOA.
PRESS
A DIVISION OF HAY HOUSE

Balboa Press books may be ordered through booksellers or by contacting:

Balboa Press
A Division of Hay House
1663 Liberty Drive
Bloomington, IN 47403
www.balboapress.com
1 (877) 407-4847

Because of the dynamic nature of the Internet, any web addresses or
links contained in this book may have changed since publication and
may no longer be valid. The views expressed in this work are solely those
of the author and do not necessarily reflect the views of the publisher,
and the publisher hereby disclaims any responsibility for them.

The author of this book does not dispense medical advice or prescribe the use
of any technique as a form of treatment for physical, emotional, or medical
problems without the advice of a physician, either directly or indirectly. The
intent of the author is only to offer information of a general nature to help
you in your quest for emotional and spiritual well-being. In the event you use
any of the information in this book for yourself, which is your constitutional
right, the author and the publisher assume no responsibility for your actions.

Print information available on the last page.

ISBN: 978-1-5043-9972-2 (sc)
ISBN: 978-1-5043-9971-5 (e)

Library of Congress Control Number: 2018902746

Balboa Press rev. date: 03/12/2018

Contents

Introduction

Many years ago, as a veterinary student, I had a respected professor who admonished us for "anthropomorphising unduly", which meant that we were not to attribute human characteristics to our animal patients. Over forty years later, I must disagree with that viewpoint. In fact, I believe it is the animals who bring us closer to our humanity, if we follow their example.

In these days of increased world hatred and violence, racism and bigotry, discrimination and intolerance, I think we must look to the animals. They don't care about skin colour, gender, religious beliefs or political affiliation. They do care about love, kindness, compassion, acceptance and joy. These are the only things that matter in truth.

We need to look at the animals through better eyes, so we can look at each other through better eyes.

The animals on these pages have been my inspiration. May they do the same for you.

"If you have men who will exclude any of God's creatures from the shelter of compassion and pity, you will have men who will deal likewise with their fellow men."

St. Francis of Assisi

Projects of the heart are never accomplished alone.

This one is thanks to my Earth Angel Loretta, for her years of gently nudging me to write; to Sandi, my soul sister for just being; to Peter, my husband, for his proofreading, editing and technical wizardry, but mostly for his love and tenderness for me, and for this project of my heart. Finally thanks especially to the animals, my greatest spiritual teachers.

Mia

Her name was MIA. She was a big beautiful Kuvasz, and life was always on her terms. She was the protector of her farm. She liked most people, a few dogs, and would pursue a coyote or a cat if it trespassed her boundaries. She had love in her heart for a Chosen Few.

Up to age nine, she had the usual mishaps; eating something she shouldn't, hurting her back as she crouched to go through her favourite culvert. Then at ten, as I watched the increasingly drunken sailor walk of her back end, I had to tell Donna, her devoted person, that I was sure she had the canine equivalent of ALS in humans, known as degenerative myelopathy.

It causes a progressive paralysis from behind, moving forward, to eventually end in death from respiratory paralysis. There is no cure. There are some unproven medicines and therapies to help slow down the advancing evil, and Donna was willing to try just about anything.

We both knew that when Mia could no longer walk, we would need to make tough decisions. We both had our doubts about Miss Mi, and her acceptance of carts and wheels that are available now for dogs that cannot walk. Also the care-taking of a 110 lb. dog's bladder and bowels becomes enormously difficult. I told Donna that we would cross each bridge when we came to it.

It was always about Mi's quality of life. So we began the twice, then three times, weekly infrared therapy, which helped for secondary muscle stiffness and soreness; drugs, supplements, and homeopathics to slow this damn thing. At each treatment, we started with a belly rub. There were days when I thought we were winning, especially if she actually tried to walk from the barn to the house, when she saw my car. Some days she would still go for walks to the pond with Donna, but as October came, the walks became fewer, although she seemed less depressed than I feared.

Her world power was shrinking, but she seemed to be serene. Donna had decided that if and when Mi could no longer walk at all, we would euthanize her. Both of us dreaded that day, but we agreed it was the right thing to do. Mia kept fooling us though. She did not eat for a day and not move very far without assistance. I thought we were at the end, and then she trotted wobbly down the hill to me under her own steam, almost with that smile on her face that said, "See I can still do this." On the bad days, Donna had totally understandable meltdowns. Caring for a beloved animal, with a serious affliction, is no less stressful than caring for a human.

On Wednesday, November 5, I arrived for Mia's usual treatment. I wondered how many more there would be. She had not moved much since yesterday. When I arrived, she was lying on the lawn by the house. I put my equipment in the house with the intention of going back out to help Mi inside. Armed with my trusty towel as a support sling, I opened the door to the house and there she was, having arrived, again, under her own steam. As she came for our usual kiss, cuddle, and treatment, I had no idea it was our last. An appointment delayed Donna, so for a while it was just Mi and I. It's always so peaceful when it's just you and the animal you're working on.

A lovely quiet symbiosis develops between the two of you. We finished our hour, and Donna agreed I would return the following day.

My drive home is about an hour long. I was 30 minutes away, when the cellphone rang. All I heard was a sobbing wail in the background, the kind of sound that accompanies a deeply tragic and shocking event. It is pain that resonates to your core. As it drove onto the farm, a two-ton truck had hit Mia. She was whimpering; Donna was coming undone.

The 30-minute return was done in 20 minutes with that strange slow motion adrenaline characteristic of emergencies. What kept going through my mind was that Mia had orchestrated this horror to end her situation. It was hard to fathom, and I repeatedly asked the angels for their help and guidance. Everyone had gathered at the top of the driveway. As Donna sobbed, I held it together while I examined Mia. I knew that massive internal bleeding had occurred and that there was nothing to do but end her pain.

Through her tears, Donna agreed. As I ran back to the car for my euthanasia equipment, I heard Donna say, "You better bring a shot for me too." When the deed was done, the young truck driver helped me put Mia in the back of my car. I needed to reassure him that this was not his fault, just wrong place, wrong time. While Mia and the universe may have orchestrated this, I knew she would not want to assign blame. She had created an opportunity for forgiveness among the remaining humans. Before the young man left, he tearfully hugged Donna. She told him truthfully and gently that this was not his fault, and that Mia didn't think so either.

I know that Universal forces lined up that afternoon because Mia felt that her work in physical form was done. Her love and compassion for Donna removed the need for an active, awful decision of elective euthanasia, which can often riddle humans with guilt and second-guessing. As always, Mia did it her way. She still guides us. When I am still; I know she is, I am, we all are...

As humans we usually think that we are in control of life events. Sometimes we are, but sometimes an animals' free will and soul choice over-ride ours. Our animals are not lesser than, just different.

Angelique

I had the dogs outside in the yard, late one fall afternoon. I felt gratitude for the warmth of the sun, when a monarch butterfly, literally, fell at my feet. I love monarchs. They often appear to me as an angel sign that a loved one, who has passed, is near. It calms me.

As I looked closer at this incredible creature, I realized she had injuries. There were, literally, gaping holes in her wings with the edge of one bent and almost broken.

I took her inside, placed her in a box on a pink blanket, offering her sugar water. There was no interest. I put a tiny drop of Rescue Remedy on her head, then decided to leave her in peace for twenty minutes. When I returned, she was brighter and crawled onto my hand. I sat on the floor with her for the night, waking every few hours, expecting her to have passed.

Morning came; she was alive, still not wanting to leave my hand. Because it was beautiful outside that day, I thought she might eat at the remaining milkweed in the lane. She didn't. Her injuries made balancing difficult. She continued to cling to my hand. I knew that she was not going to survive.

I had to go on calls that day, but knew I could not leave her. In her box on her pink blanket, she rode on the passenger seat. With my hand over her, she received Reiki and the assurance that she was not alone.

I have always prayed for the grace to be with my creatures when they transition, whether it is the active process of a humane euthanasia, or the unfolding of a natural event. I think this is a part of honouring physical life, be it dog, cat, horse, human or butterfly. It is not the end, rather, a new beginning. Angelique took her final breath as I parked the car in the driveway at the end of our day together.

I cried as much for her as for any other creature that I have loved. Her delicate strength, grace and peaceful passing inspired me. She made me realize the importance of presence for end of life issues, no matter the species. It is the gentle quietness of holding a hand, a paw, a tiny butterfly leg. It is the silent stillness being there with someone. This is life, especially at the physical end. Being present. Nothing to do, but allowing spirit to be.

Gracie

Sometimes you have to ask for help even when it goes against the grain.

Gracie was one of the carport kittens that we rescued when we moved to Second line. She was the only one at five weeks and for the rest of her life to maintain her feral nature. She liked other cats, but had a complete disregard for humans. Despite always speaking to her gently, she shot me a look of disdain and walked away. We lived in a working standoff.

One day when she was about six years old, she stood at the edge of the bathroom and stared at me. She had a tired look rather than the usual malevolence. I thought that maybe, just maybe, she had begun to need some human interaction. At that point she turned and walked away. The next day, she made a pointed venture into the bathroom.

For the first time ever, she sat at my feet. It was then I realized that she was sick. She wobbled. Her coat looked suddenly dreadful and spiky. Her glassy eyes said, "I need your help even though I don't want it." My heart sank. We had just lost her brother Siem and I wasn't ready for a second one so soon. For the first time since her rescue I picked her up. She did not resist. I put her in a cage and started fluids thinking she was not going to survive whatever had started her kidneys to fail.

Everyday for three weeks she let me treat and even syringe feed her. Each day the low growl was a little louder and more insistent until she decided she was fine, thank you very much. She ate on her own again and didn't need me poking her with any more needles.

I opened the cage door; she trotted out; stopped to groom a paw; and shot me that familiar scornful look that was now maybe a little bit softer than before.

I think in hindsight Gracie mourned her brother Siem's passing several weeks earlier. They spent a lot of time together. They were friends. As with humans, grief takes an emotional and subsequent physical toll. I believe animals experience discord and stress in their world dynamic when there is big loss. They often seem, however, to overcome these losses faster than we do. They seem to fill in the heart holes better than we do, not because they are lesser beings but quite the opposite.

I often think they are more spiritually evolved. They seem to let go of emotional baggage far better than humans. There is more openness to clearing their heart heavy pain. They have an ability to move forward better. That quality is another aspiration for me.

Jeddy

J eddy was a redhead. A domestic short-hair with eyes that looked right through you, to see what was in your heart. She also had a wicked sense of humour.

Loretta's husband was not keen to have the cat in their bedroom at night, so the door was shut, and Jeddy found a spot elsewhere in the house. At one point their neighbourhood experienced a series of break-ins. It was a small community, and people were nervous. In the middle of one night during this, Loretta heard a door rattle. When it happened again a few minutes later, she awakened John, thinking that an intruder had entered the house. Armed with a baseball bat, John arose and searched the house while Loretta called 911. The police arrived, but found nothing.

Exhausted, in bed and almost asleep; they heard the door rattle. John grabbed the bat, threw open the bedroom door, in time to see Jeddy finish batting the doorknob and walk down the hallway. He swore she had a smile on her face. John's exasperated remark to Loretta was, "You can't tell my friends that I called the cops on a cat!"

Over the years since then, Jeddy and I had some lovely encounters during laser treatments for her arthritis. She was the one who taught me that animals know how much treatment they want and where. Jeddy would lie while I lasered her, moving her body to where she wanted the laser beam to treat her. I had very little to do but watch and listen to Jeddy tell me what felt best. It was amazing to watch her get up and walk away after exactly sixty minutes of treatment every time.

When it was time for her to leave this mortal plain, Jeddy was adamant that she wanted to do this herself. She had conveyed this to Loretta's sister, Jackie, a talented animal communicator. I knew I had to honour this, while eliminating any possibility of Jeddy suffering. Loretta and I agreed to heavy sedation repeated as needed until Jeddy could leave her broken little body. If there was any distress, I would intervene with an IV.

It was the most beautiful, gentle, and loving afternoon passing in which I have had the privilege to participate. Loretta sang to her, reminisced with Jackie and I about her antics over the years, along with all the love given and received. For a while, Jeddy seemed to move back and forth between here and beyond. Her heartbeat and respiration stopped, only to restart. I was about to reach for the IV as both Jackie and Loretta said, "Why isn't she going?". Then the angelic penny dropped. I said to Loretta, "Is there something you used to call her when she was a kitten?" She nodded through her tears, nuzzled her girl and said, "I love you little peanut." Almost instantaneously Jeddy was gone.

She took her last breath at 4:44 that day. It wasn't until years later that I realized the significance of that time. It meant the Angels were present in full force to carry her on her way to her next journey.

According to Jackie, Jeddy called me Dr. Love. While at the time that embarrassed me, because it felt a bit like a radio talk-show moniker, I now embrace the sentiment. Jeddy has honoured and humbled me. After all, love really is all there is, but we can enjoy ourselves along the way.

Jenny and Gibbs

The seriousness of this book had created a bog. Many tales of lessons and loss weighed heavily. I went to Doreen Virtue's Fairy Card deck for advice. The laughter card appeared. I decided it was time to write a story about joy.

Two months after I lost the last greyhound brother, Dodger, grief had consumed me. I had decided no more dogs. I would simply devote myself to Norma Jean, who at fourteen, deserved my undivided attention. Then a rescue group called. They needed a vet reference for a client wishing to adopt one of their dogs. As the conversation continued, Deanna told me about her rescue work and her particular frustration with a mother Husky/Shepherd cross and her pup.

Despite a massive internet campaign, no one wanted to even foster them. The mom had lived under a shed on a construction site since late fall. The site manager brought her food and blankets which she dragged under the shed. She would not, however, let him get close. The weather was dreadful that November and December with horribly cold temperatures and accumulating snow. It was now January.

This lovely man brought food every day, through the holidays, including Christmas Day. Roast beef and ham was the usual fare. She still would not let him get close. As the calendar closed in on mid January, a small body stuck his nose out from under the shed. She had a puppy! Deanna and her team succeeded in the rescue. First the pup, then mom, who willingly followed.

They were currently at the SPCA, with the idea of separating them for easier adoption. I empathized with Deanna's predicament. Their possible separation horrified me. I lay awake all night thinking about the two of them and what they must have been through. It was as if something overtook me. There was not much logical reasoning about this. I simply knew I had to call Deanna in the morning. I asked to take both of them. They arrived three days later.

Jenny Shepherd bonded instantly. I knew the moment we met that it was not for the first time. I don't know the circumstances of how she came to be at that construction site, and I don't want to know. While it breaks my heart to think of what she may have been through, she has overcome her past. She sets another example for me. Her resilience and loyalty is only matched by the joy in her eyes when we play ball. It is her greatest pleasure in life, and always makes me smile.

I am so grateful to the angels for sending Jenny and Gibbs to me. He may have gnawed the couch at the time of this writing, but I am still smiling. The fairies tell me that it is good for me.

Jetson

J etson was a dangerous dog. An Australian Cattle dog with soulful brown eyes whose insanity switch engaged in a flash, especially by human adolescent males in baseball caps.

He came to me shortly after he attempted to intercept a paperboy, who had physically and innocently stepped between Jet and Mrs. H, his current owner. She wanted to return him to the Humane Society. I knew that he would not emotionally survive another home change, let alone a bureaucratic euthanasia decision. At four years old, with a serious case of canine PTSD, he came to live with us.

His devotion to me was instantaneous, matched only by the love of catching his frisbee. He travelled with me as I went on calls. At gas stations, he invariably tried to dive through the windshield to attack the young male attendant (in the days before self-serve). My biceps worked hard as I strained to keep him from going through the glass. He improved with time, but I always needed to exercise caution around people and other animals.

One day, Jet was with me on a frequent trip to a lovely part of rural Ontario, just Northwest of Toronto. I parked the car, attached his leash, and we went for a walk, savouring a gorgeous, late summer day. It was just Jet and I on a country road without another soul around, except the wildlife, when suddenly, a vehicle slowly approached us. It was an ominous, beat-up, grey sedan of unknown origin. At approximately 500 feet away, my heart pounded as I prayed for safety. This was in the days before I knew to invoke Archangel Michael's presence, but I know in hindsight that he was there anyway; he and my protector Jet.

The car crept alongside of us. I did not stop as the driver rolled down the passenger window and asked if I knew where the Nottawasaga River was. No, was my curt answer as Jet and I walked faster towards our car. I remember that my quick glance registered a man who resembled Pure Evil. I had never seen or experienced something so palpably vile.

Jet and I kept walking. He did not bark, growl or get hyper but, he shot the man a look that said, if you touch her, you will answer to me. The car stopped as Jet and I continued those last few feet to our car. We jumped in, I locked the doors and turned on the ignition. As I watched the rear view mirror, the grey evil turned around and slowly drove away.

It took a long time for my nausea to fade, and two days to stop shaking. I know that Jet saved my life that day. That man had violence in his heart. If I had been there alone or with any other dog, this story would not exist, and I would be swamp food.

I am so truly grateful to the universe and the angels for my loyal and devoted Jetson. As they say in the movies, he would have taken a bullet for me. Years later, he died in my arms, from an enlarged heart. I know it was because he had the biggest and best heart of any dog I've ever known, and he gave it all to me.

> "He is your friend, your partner, your defender, your dog.
>
> You are his life, his love, his leader.

He will be yours, faithful to the last
beat of his heart.

You owe it to him to be worthy of such
devotion."

Author Unknown

Kapnik and Yukon

One of the truly great joys of my life was howling with a wolf. This particular one was a domesticated mush-ball named Yukon; half wolf, half god-knows what, but still 230 pounds of awe-inspiring canine who could stop you in your tracks with trepidation, if you didn't know him. My visits were not initially for him, but for his mate, who was really more like an older sister to him; a very smart older sister.

Kapnik was the brainiac, part wolf, but a little smaller, about 175 pounds. She had no patience for certain things. Cats were one. At lightning speed, she chased any stray from her massive wrap-around porch. Her other pet peeve was the fish tank timer that began its cycle in the middle of the night. She apparently had had enough of its click-click sound.

Her human Mom came downstairs one morning to find the timer removed from the fish tank and systematically dismantled, piece by piece, with engineering precision. All the components were laid out as if in a floor plan. There was not a chew-mark anywhere. Several exotic fish species were present and accounted for. Kapnik lay in front of her masterpiece, snoozing, with a smile on her face, while Yukon snored on his couch in an adjoining room oblivious to his sister's brilliant exploits.

Kapnik sized you up, looked right through you and knew what was in your heart. Your intention needed to be honest. She allowed a lot under those circumstances, as we treated her for a tumour, by various means, for almost two years. If I crossed a line with what I was doing to her, she would simply lay her head over my wrist and give me her furrowed brow "stop" look. She never growled, never bit, but her message was clear. She could have literally eaten me and not left a trace. She commanded respect and I think I reciprocated. You only receive it when you give it.

Yukon was the goofball. He acted as the greeter when I arrived in those days, often three times a week. After insisting on a head and face rub, his low rumble began. That massive head would fling back and he emitted a long howl that permeated your soul. The first time I joined in, he stopped momentarily, came over, licked my face, then resumed our song. It became our ritual until the day he died.

I actually am blessed to have recorded one of our songs. I can honestly say he taught me how to truly sing from the heart. Kapnik was never a member of our howling duo until at one visit she purposely and happily brought a lovely harmony to Yukon's and my song. For a full glorious three minutes, the three of us threw our heads back and howled. It was our one and only trio.

When I saw Kapnik, two days later, she was dying. Did she know that wild and primal howl was her last chance to sing? I think so. Did she do it to give me the thrill of a lifetime? Did she do it deliberately to include me in her pack? Yes, on both counts. There is the power of music, no matter the kind, and I am truly grateful for that memory. The lessons? If something is important, do it with all your heart. Be smart, but be inclusive.

Kermie and Scotchie

Kermie is a sweet but determined Calico cat who started life in a drug house. When I rescued her, Kermie was more than a little pregnant. She was about to drop. The emergency cesarean/ spay yielded six dead kittens, but Kermie never looked back.

She recovered physically and emotionally to became the household aerialist. Life was good for her for almost three years as she enjoyed the world from her various heights. Then an accidental fall rocked her world. A neck injury had partially paralyzed her.

There was minimal hind-end mobility, but she had manageable bowel control and urine retention.

We did, and still do, physio and magnetic therapy. She loved the attention and the company, especially when Merlin, my nineteen year old wise red tabby, came into her protected space to cuddle with her. She often gave a huge sigh of relief when Merlin settled beside her, and his purring began. I started to worry about what would happen when Merlin left us. Sure enough, he passed one day, while lying with his dear friend.

Kermie coped, but there was a new sadness about her. She grieved as animals do, often in the same way as humans. Although I tried to spend more time with her, what she really needed was another four-legged soul-mate. Some of the other cats came and went from Kermie's space, but nobody filled the void until Scotchie arrived.

He is a wise and soulful butterscotch tabby who came to me because of an "inappropriate urination issue." Scotchie marked his territory at home, in addition to having a urinary tract infection. We had tried all the usual remedies, but to no avail. As his humans' frustration mounted amidst great pangs of guilt over the alternatives, I offered to take him home to see how a new environment might work. Positive results had happened with several other wee ones over the years, with the same issue, so I thought it was worth a shot.

My feeling is that if you eliminate the physical reason, such as infection or inflammation, cats mark when they are unhappy or stressed about something. That something can vary greatly. Sometimes it's an attempt to dominate in a group of animals, sometimes it's the desire of a cat to be outdoors, sometimes it's the deep emotional pain of a fractured family, as in divorce. Scotchie was none of these.

From the moment he joined the fold, he never

again used anything but a litter box. He did though, march straight to Kermie and plunk himself down next to her, quietly and gently, as if he had done this forever. I think the universe, once again, orchestrated events for his life purpose of nurturing. It continues to this day, and Kermie smiles again.

I think it is important for us to look at animal behaviour with better eyes, not just clinically, but with empathy. I know I am a better person for the awareness, for the mindfulness.

As usual, I have the animals to thank for the small and, sometimes, the big miracles.

Minerva and Persephone

I had a call one day about a stray cat hanging around a local country church. It was fall, and the caller expressed concern about a food source for her, especially as the temperatures had begun to change.

I arrived, cage in hand, to get the lay of the land. There was the very thin calico by the side of the building. She did not run, she did not approach, but she was not alone. Beside her and closer to the building wall was her doppleganger. Neither fled as I sat on the grass to see what might unfold.

After watching me with careful curiosity for a long time, the two began to move in a very purposeful and calculated way. The outside girl leaned into the other closest to the wall of the church, as they navigated the building's perimeter. When they were about ten feet from my spot, they both turned to look at me. At that point, I saw that the eyes of the one closest to the wall were fully dilated, despite the brightness of the day. She was blind!

The outside girl appeared to be her guide, literally, physically leaning into her as they walked. Clearly, they had done this for some time, because their movements were almost a dance. At one point, they stopped to rest under a tree. Guide Girl suddenly sat bolt upright and sprinted to the edge of the nearby cornfield. With lightning speed, she dispatched a mouse, carried it back to Blind Girl, allowing her to eat first. The caring and kindness was humbling to watch.

I knew the angels had led me to rescue them, but this was not going to be a slam-dunk. I took advantage of the fact that Blind Girl ate first. I set my gentle cage trap with tuna, then prayed that Guide Girl would be hungry enough to investigate.

Rescue is, more often than not, about patience. It took an hour and forty-five minutes before she decided to warily walk into the trap and spring it closed. Remarkably she did not panic, but as she stared at me, I heard her say, "This is a package deal. Don't forget my mother."

I quietly talked to Blind Girl as I approached. She didn't move. Within inches, I put my hand out to her nose. She sniffed and put her head in my hand. We both felt an enormous sense of relief. She let me put her in a cage without any fuss. Guide Girl was calm during this. I think she was grateful that life would, hopefully, be easier from now on.

When I finally examined them, it seemed that Blind Girl was older and the mother/daughter scenario fit. Guide Girl was about two years old. I wondered about the length of mom's blindness and their arrangement. There was no way of knowing, but that didn't really matter.

Over the years they lived their lives happily and safely, indoors with me, always together, always grooming each other. Blind Girl navigated the house on her own extremely well, once she learned the layout, but Guide Girl was never far away, always ready to help.

Mother and daughter became Minerva and Persephone respectively. They were the Roman goddess of wisdom and the Greek goddess of springtime flowers. Years later, Persephone died suddenly. Minerva followed two days later.

Teamwork and trust here and beyond.

Miss Peony

There was something at the side of the road. We backed towards it and there, to my astonishment, was a domestic rabbit; not panic-stricken but quite content. She let me collect her without the usual rabbit kick struggle and lay very quietly and calmly in my arms. This occurred at the top end of the country road on which we lived. She was on the heavily wooded side. Why on earth was she out here?

As I peered down the embankment, I saw the rabbit cage at the bottom. It had broken into several pieces. Someone had thrown her cage and contents from a vehicle. I knew the tears needed to wait; if I succumbed to them I was of no use to her. I handed her to Peter, and went down the hill to see if there was another of her kind, or worse yet babies. There were no others, but it was remarkable that she was even alive. The cage had struck a substantial tree limb before flying apart.

Somehow she survived the fall and managed to climb the hill to the road. Fortunately, she had not been there for too long. I knew this was not an accident. There was a stop sign twenty feet from where she sat, so a driver knew she had fallen off as they stopped, if there had indeed been a load imbalance. Aside from some hind-end bruising, she was physically uninjured.

I have found it astonishing how animals rebound from trauma and abuse, whether emotional, physical or both. Once in loving homes, they become role models for living in the moment. Miss Peony did just that. I named her after one of my favourite flowers which bloomed in profusion as we drove her home that day.

She continued to blossom for the rest of her time with us, enjoying gentle sparring with her cat friends, a head of romaine lettuce and yogurt treats daily. Rabbit pellets were a no-go, but chin rubs were rapturous.

Time is always too short with our wondrous creatures. One morning, I found her gone in her cage, without warning or time for goodbyes. While broken with grief, I was grateful for our brief time together. What did I learn from this gentle sweet soul? Live for today. None of us really know how long we have in this physical place.

Let us not waste our time on regret, sadness, resentment or lack of forgiveness.

Our animal angels know we have better purposes to achieve.

Molly and TooToo

Molly was the first outside cat to appear when we moved to Second line. She looked about two years old. She let me stroke that pretty, dilute tortoiseshell head briefly. She was also more than a little pregnant. She came for food every day. Try as I might to entice her into a live trap, she had disdain for it.

As her belly grew, I asked for angel intervention but, apparently, there was another plan afoot. Molly disappeared for four days. She must have had the kittens; I scoured the property but, no Molly and no babies. Now worry set in. She hadn't come for food, which she needed to maintain her strength for nursing. Had she had a delivery problem? What if? What if? I managed to create several disaster scenarios, until I surrendered and said to the angels, "Please just keep her safe."

Then she appeared. Thin, gaunt and a little wobbly, she looked exhausted. As I stroked her, she put her head in my hand with a huge sigh. I took a deep breath, picked her up and brought her into the house. The bathroom became her domain after her spay and recovery from whatever she had gone through. The most she revealed to my extraordinary animal communicator, Jackie, was that, "her kitten wasn't strong enough and that she didn't want to talk about this anymore."

She lived in the bathroom for the rest of her days with her friend TooToo whose gentle and generous nature became a reliable constant for Molly. They curled up together in Molly's bed, arms wrapped around each other purring so loudly it rattled the house. BFF, I think, is the current terminology that applies.

Over the years, Molly developed a very troubling stomatitis, which is an inflammation involving the mouth. It made eating difficult for her until we found the right holistic treatment. She did well with TooToo's support until she went into kidney failure that I couldn't help her body combat. TooToo and I knew it was time to let her go. Being present is one of the biggest animal lessons for me.

TooToo embodied that as she lay wrapped around Molly purring into the rafters as I gave my dear sweet, gentle girl the sedative that is part of my euthanasia protocol. Molly didn't flinch or object, which is always my indicator that I'm doing the right thing. Before the final IV needle, with Molly now fully sedated, TooToo gave her a final head bump. Then she stood, moved to the door, looked at me as if to say you can finish this now, I'll be outside. There she sat, quietly, reflectively until Molly passed.

It has been said that for animals, death is similar to walking through a doorway. While I know they grieve physical loss just as we do, most of them seem to have a better awareness of that other side; a better acceptance of it because they seem to know it is real. Listen to a good animal communicator, and you'll know animals comprehend better than we do.

Sybil

S ybil had a split personality. A small but mighty domestic short-hair who could head-bump you one minute, or tear your skin open the next, without real rhyme or reason; just the whim of the moment. It's not surprising, considering her early days. She had some itchy, open sore, skin issues as a young cat.

Her humans had wrapped her in duct tape, attempting to stop the constant scratching and licking that kept them awake at night. When she landed on my exam table in her grey body-cast, it took everything I had not to weep. I held it together as I asked if they preferred I keep her. Their relief was palpable. When they left the clinic, Sandi and I tried to figure out how to remove the damned stuff. We did and Sybil healed.

She lived life on her terms until at fourteen, she developed breast cancer. She was too old for surgery, so I took a deep breath. Would she condescend to eat her food with a combination of herbs and supplements, to help her immune system cope as best it could? Twice a day for sixteen months, she ate everything, everyday. She was a willing participant until the day she stopped eating period. The tumour had gone through phases of shrinkage and staying the same. Now, it was marginally bigger.

As I kissed her goodnight after that day of food refusal, I thought of alternative treatments or food for her. I slept on it, but my Sybil had other ideas. When I awoke in the morning and put my hand down to her bed, the usual head bump did not happen. I sat bolt upright and realized to my horror that she had passed in the night. So Sybil, so her way.

She was the denizen of self respect. We must be caretakers of our animal companions, and we must also respect their right to choose how they exit this mortal plain. I acknowledge how emotionally painful this can be. It is one of my life's biggest tests, but I aspire to achieve that acceptance along with the grief. After all, we only grieve if we have lost someone we love, whether they have two legs or four. It makes us brighter spiritual lights.

Zeke

I knew I had to tell Zeke's story, but I struggled with which spiritual aspiration to attribute to him. I realized he embodied and taught me all of them, during his physical time with me and beyond. Forgiveness, kindness, compassion, gratitude and love. He and his lessons are eternal, as so are all of us.

In 1999, I met the canine love of my life. Ezekiel, the Greyhound, was nine years old, and the sweetest, gentlest, kindest, most compassionate and nurturing soul I have ever known.

We came together because his owners wanted me to euthanize him. He had recently developed epilepsy and soiled their cream coloured carpet when he seizured. That was not acceptable to the humans. I seriously considered suggesting they contact someone else to do this, but the angels insisted that I go.

When I arrived, Zeke's depression was palpable. This was not a case of an animal's grace, acceptance and gratitude for the human decision, when the time for transition is truly right. This felt all wrong. As my mind raced to figure out how I could make Zeke and I disappear in a puff of magical smoke, his people said, "Would you take him with you? We don't want it done here." No tears, no emotion, just a matter of fact request.

"Absolutely", I responded trying not to belie my incredulity at the turn of events, until I realized it was late Friday afternoon of a long weekend. I had no phenobarbital on hand to control his seizures. As I walked him to the car, my mind raced to solve this problem. I said to the angels, "Guys, find me some phenobarb, please." Almost immediately, one of the humans emerged from the house and said, "Can you use this for someone else?" It was his bottle of phenobarb.

Thanking her quickly, I put Zeke in the car and drove away. Two blocks away, I pulled over and cried. The angels had worked their magic and, I learned the meaning of trust in the universe.

Despite taking my newest family member home, all was not happy for Zeke. For the rest of that long weekend, he was morose. He wouldn't eat, despite all my efforts at trying to win him over with food and love. I knew he felt abandoned, probably betrayed and grief stricken at what his humans had done. They were the only family he had ever known since he was a pup. He was not a racetrack rescue, as is the usual situation with Greyhounds.

My Bach Flower remedies and roast beef had no impact. I wondered if putting him down was what he wanted and the right thing to do. Amidst my tears and distress, the phone rang as the two of us sat in my office. Zeke faced away from me, refusing to make eye contact, while I was drowning in sadness for this beautiful boy. I didn't pick up the phone, the answering machine clicked on to broadcast the message from Zeke's people. All they wanted to know was if everything had gone well, nothing more.

When Zeke heard her voice, he stood, turned his head to the phone, listening intently. The call ended, he came over to me and put his head in my lap with a huge sigh. It was as if he knew that part of his life was truly gone. Would he willingly move beyond the hurt to go forward?

He let me stroke his head for the longest time, then he walked to the door into the main house, trotted to the kitchen and stood looking at Peter making a peanut butter sandwich. A piece of the sandwich dropped to the floor. Zekie bent that long giraffe neck down to the floor, sniffed, then very delicately ate the morsel. Hoping we might be on a roll, we made him his own sandwich, cut into "garden party cubes" and watched smiling as he worked his way through the whole thing. He looked lighter, emotionally and spiritually. I thought to myself that the gift of forgiveness benefits the forgiver the most.

While peanut butter sandwiches became a staple as a first breakfast, commercial dog food was an absolute no-go. By accident, which I really believe was divine intervention, I was out early one morning and starving as I drove by one of our local fast food places. While this wasn't something I would normally do, I got toast for me and a very unhealthy egg and sausage breakfast for Zekie. Might there be some appetite stimulation with this semi-awful junk food? It worked and after gobbling it down, I swear my boy was smiling. He wasn't done.

Then began what I lovingly referred to as the tantrum stamp. He rocked back and forth on his front feet, left to right, with a gentle stamp of each foot, because he was still hungry. Then we served third breakfast, which was the chicken stew mixture the other the dogs ate. This became his daily routine for the six years that I was blessed to have him in my life. It was well into year three before I told the fast-food ladies who ate second breakfast.

They saw us parking the car and had it ready by the time we entered the store. When Valerie finally asked if this was my mid-morning snack, I took a deep breath and told her the truth. I have always been sensitive about my animals. As a child and even now, people including family, have found my attraction to animals weird. I have endured teasing with the Dr. Doolittle references and sometimes with much more hurtful words.

Valerie, a hardworking woman in her late twenties, had that no-nonsense edge to her that comes from life's school of hard knocks. I didn't know her story, but my intuition told me she endured some serious stuff. With her eyes welling up she said, "That's one lucky dog", as she handed me the food with an unsolicited order of toast inside. Human kindness appears when you least expect it. Thank you, Zekie, for another lesson.

I took Zeke on calls with me, partly because of his fear of abandonment, partly because he liked the attention as he occupied the car's entire back seat, and partly because, every ten to twelve weeks, his seizures happened like clockwork. Then he needed constant monitoring.

They were violent, full body, spastic convulsions that happened over six to twelve hours, despite his conventional medicine and homeopathics. It took him a day and a half to fully recover. Life virtually stopped. I cancelled or postponed appointments. Every client knew why, and almost all understood. I remain grateful to that core clientele for their kindness, compassion and non-judgement.

During our years together, our nurturing couch potato raised a litter of three kittens. They needed to be confined to our bedroom because of a congenital neurological issue that affected their mobility. Bondar, Simon and Porthos curled along Zeke's belly and purred to the rafters. Sometimes, this lasted for hours. Our Zekie was not a high energy dog, except for his power surges. At a blistering speed, he ran the backyard, turning on a dime, leaving the other dogs in his wake. While I abhor the practice of Greyhound racing, it was in his breeding. It was, however, easy to appreciate his grace and speed when he willingly turned it on.

Because he spent so much time in bed, our bed that is, we exchanged a double for a king size. He developed a habit of laying between us, not lengthwise, but horizontally. Peter and I each had our allotted six inches of mattress, Zeke had the rest. We laughingly waved goodnight to each other across the happily snoozing expanse of Greyhound.

His seizures continued over the years with a little less frequency, but not any less drama. One day he came upstairs with me to the bathroom, which was directly at the top of a straight but narrow staircase. As I brushed my teeth, he went into full seizure mode. Before I could grab his collar, he catapulted backward towards the stairs. They say that accidents always appear to happen in slow motion. This was no exception. I watched in horror as the double backward somersault unfolded. It seemed incredible that he landed at the bottom of fourteen steps, upright on all fours, without making body contact along the way. He should have broken every bone in his body, including his neck. There was not a scratch anywhere on him. The angels had him in super bubble wrap that day.

At fourteen, I relished his now beautifully greying muzzle, when he started to stumble on his back feet. As his seizure frequency reduced to virtually nothing over the next year, he became unable to walk as degenerative myelopathy took over his body. As with Mia, the canine equivalent of ALS was upon us.

He was the trooper, not me. He still went on calls with me, regal as ever, as Peter and I carried him to and from the car on his comforter. Every four hours, day and night we turned him to prevent muscle and tissue damage, from being in one position too long. Bowel and bladder issues also needed attention. With a distinctive little whine, he always let me know, that he needed my help.

He still ate with joy, and he loved the attention. Considering our beginnings, I am so grateful and proud of getting him to fifteen. I had my meltdowns, often from the sleep deprivation, but I learned the fine art of the power-nap. We managed as we settled into the "new norm", as only chronic illness can provide. Those levels of change happen with declining health.

When you are in a steady state of routine, you are grateful for that consistency. It provides comfort, even when you know in the back of your mind that it is not going to last forever, no matter how much you want it to. One day as I was laying with him, just looking into those kind and gentle eyes, I told him I didn't know how I was ever going to be able to help him when the time came. In other words, I didn't know how I was going to be able to euthanize him when it was time.

Despite the fact it was what I did professionally, and had always mustered the strength for other beloved animals of my own, Zekie was different. I knew I couldn't do it. As I said the words, he looked at me lovingly through my tears and gave me a head bump.

The norm continued for a few more months, until one day he did not eat his breakfast. This was the first food refusal since those very early days and I had that sickening feeling in my soul that we were at the end. He was serene. I was panic stricken. I needed to clear my head and regain some semblance of composure, so I left him for a moment to collect myself in my office. It was maybe three minutes, when Peter came to me and said, "You need to come." I raced to the bedroom to find my beautiful boy gone. True to his noble and compassionate self, he spared me the agony of having to intervene. My only regret is that in my selfishness, I wasn't with him when he took his last breath. I knew the angels were though. Although it was not the correct time, the clock flashed 4:44 when I walked into the room.

He is the dog I miss everyday. He is the one for whom I cry when I see a Greyhound on the street or in a park. He is the one who embodies the best of the best. He is the one who embodies love.

My friend Loretta sent me this anonymous poem. It is the essence of Zeke's gift to me. I am so grateful and blessed that if my heart is a fraction as generous and loving as his, then as Wayne Dyer has said, "I am better than I used to be."

"It came to me that every time I lose a dog, they take a piece of my heart with them and every new dog who comes into my life gifts me with a piece of their heart.

If I live long enough, all the components Of my heart will be dog And I will become as generous and loving As they are."

Anonymous

Printed in the United States
By Bookmasters